KNOTS
and
RIGS

DICK LEWERS

with line illustrations by the author

REED

REED BOOKS PTY LTD
3/470 Sydney Road Balgowlah NSW 2093

First published 1969
Revised and enlarged 1972
Reprinted 1973, 1976 (twice), 1977, 1978, 1980
This metricated edition 1981
Reprinted 1983
1984
1985
1987
1988
1990

National Library of Australia
Cataloguing-in-Publication Data

Lewers, Dick
  Fishing knots and rigs.
  ISBN 0 7301 0121 5
  1. Fishing knots – Handbooks, manuals, etc.
  I. Title.
799.1

Set by Showbill Pty Ltd, Sydney

Printed in Singapore for
Imago Productions (F.E.) Pte. Ltd.

Contents

Preface

This preface is necessarily brief. You haven't bought this book because of a desire to philosophise. You want to learn about knots and rigs suitable for catching different species of fish, and I've set myself the pleasant task of showing you.

In the illustrations that follow, you will notice the letters "E" and "S". Turn to Figure 1 and you will see what I mean. It is important you understand what they stand for.

The letter "E" is used to designate the end of a line or rope; to the sailor, this end, being known as the "running end". The letter "S" is used to designate the remainder of the line or rope and, correctly, is known as the "standing part".

I hope the hints throughout this book will help you. Good luck with your fishing—may you frequently enjoy a meal of self-caught fish!

1 Fishing Knots

Knots are a fundamental of the sport of angling, and the angler blessed with a knowledge of their intricacies and the ability to tie them is, in ninety-nine cases out of a hundred, a successful angler.

Line to Hook

The casual fisherman need only learn how to tie two knots—the Blood Knot, and the Half Blood Knot.

The Half Blood Knot (Figs. 1 and 2)

Let's start with the latter—the Half Blood Knot—a basic knot used to tie nylon line to a hook, swivel, or ring. An extremely simple knot to tie, it is one of the most important and frequently used knots in the angler's repertoire. The process is simple.

Pass the end through the swivel or hook eye and wind it around the main line at least four times, returning the end through the loop formed immediately above the eye of the hook, (Step 1, Fig. 1). When the knot is drawn tight, it will ride against the hook as shown in Step 2.

Some anglers pass the end through the eye twice before winding it around the line, but I doubt the advantage of this.

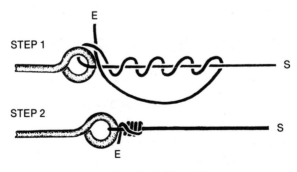

Fig. 1. The Half Blood Knot

In fact, I regard with suspicion the compression of that part of the end crushed against the eye of the hook by the extra loop.

At this point it should be made clear that any knot tied in a nylon line will affect, by reducing, its tensile strength. Certain knots have less effect than others; the comparison usually being described as a percentage of the unknotted strength of the line.

The knot you have just tied—the Half Blood Knot—reduces the static strength of your line by approximately 4 per cent.

In other words, if the breaking strength of your line were rated at 45 kg, it would be reduced to approximately 44 kg by the tying of a Half Blood Knot.

Expressed in another way, a line in which the Half Blood Knot has been tied, has its strength reduced to 96 per cent of the unknotted line.

If this reduction in strength worries you, be consoled by the fact that this is the strongest of the knots used for the purpose mentioned.

However, having learned to tie this knot, you are faced with the problem of slippage and, let's face it, the Half Blood Knot *will* slip under steady constant pressure. In fact, some anglers using this knot believe it to have broken when, in actual fact, it has slipped undone!

The solution is extremely simple, and is known as "locking" the knot. Reference to Fig. 2 will show how this is done by returning the running end of the line through the large loop it forms with the standing part of the line. The "running end", incidentally, is the name given to the free end of the line whilst the "standing part" is the remainder or main part of the line.

Fig. 2. The Locked Half Blood Knot

The Hangman's Noose (Fig. 3)

The late Gary Chapman introduced me to this knot, which is both strong and easy to tie.

Excellent for attaching line to brass ring or swivel, it can also be used for hooks as shown in Fig. 3.

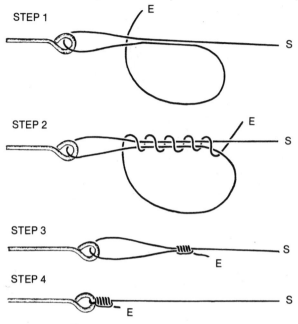

STEP 1

STEP 2

STEP 3

STEP 4

Fig. 3. The Hangman's Noose

Whilst its formation is easily followed, I should perhaps point out that having accomplished Step 2 the knot is drawn tight as in Step 3, and then worked down the line until it beds against the ring or hook eye (Step 4).

This knot bears a close resemblance to a hangman's noose and, macabre thought, is designed to hold just as securely. Its knot strength is on a par with the Locked Half Blood Knot.

Snoozing (Fig. 4)

It has been said that a good fisherman is only so when he has mastered the art of snoozing a hook! Whether you believe this or not is of little import but, should you have ambitions, then close attention to the diagrams will achieve them.

Having mastered the tying of a snood ("snoozing" is the "doing"; "snood" is the result), you can tie any hook to a line, whether it be an eyed or flatted hook. With eyed hooks,

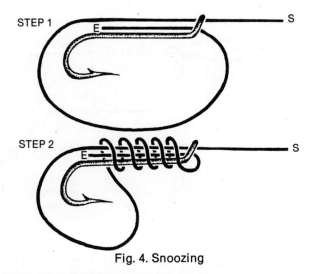

Fig. 4. Snoozing

personal preference will dictate whether the line is passed through the eye before tying. It really is immaterial.

The snood is superior in knot strength to most other knots, and will never work loose.

The Two-Circle Turtle Knot (Fig. 5)

Having now disposed of the most basic knots, let's try and increase your repertoire.

Whilst the Half Blood Knot featured earlier is excellent for attaching line to brass ring, swivel, or straight-eyed hooks, it may not be preferred by the user of the turned-down or turned-up eye hook.

This, I feel, is because most careful anglers like to have their line lying parallel to the shank of the hook, despite the fact the turned-up or turned-down eye of a hook is designed to ensure an optimum line of penetration, i.e. in the event of a strike the hook point is at its best penetrating angle when the line is tied to the eye and not around the shank.

The Two-Circle Turtle Knot, with a knot strength of 62 per cent, ensures this state of parallelism.

The tie is quite simple. Having passed the line through the eye of the hook, allow the hook, temporarily, to run up the line out of the way. Then form two complete loops with the running end as shown in Step 1, Fig. 5.

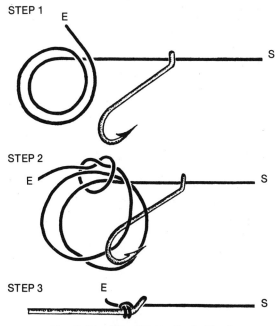

STEP 1

STEP 2

STEP 3

Fig. 5. The Two-Circle Turle Knot

Holding the two loops between the thumb and second finger of the left hand, tie a simple overhand knot around both as in Step 2. The thumb and forefinger of the left hand will assist you greatly here, even though the thumb is already in use holding the two loops.

Next, slide the hook down the line and pass the barb through the two large loops (Step 2).

By pulling on the standing part and the running end at the same time, you can draw the knot tight so that it beds in snug beneath the turned down eye.

The end can then be trimmed to within 2 mm of the knot.

The Centauri Knot (Fig. 6)

I was first shown this knot by Carl Dignam of Lord Howe Island, New South Wales, whilst fishing from his superb boat *B. Centauri*. Carl does not claim to have originated the knot, but confesses to preferring it above any other. As we used it whilst successfully fighting kingfish to 20 kg and small sharks to 22 kg on lines down to 2 kg breaking strength, it proved its efficiency by not failing once.

Not having seen it published elsewhere, I see no reason why it shouldn't be related to Carl, so I've called it the Centauri Knot—with apologies to the originator.

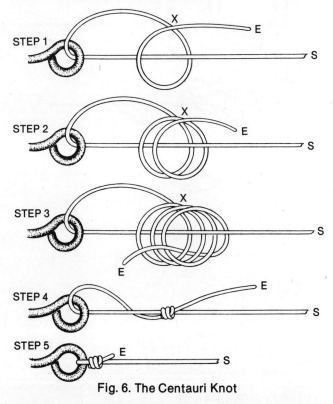

Fig. 6. The Centauri Knot

Fig. 6 shows the line being attached to the eye of a hook—or swivel, if you like. The end is passed BEHIND the standing part, then forward and back to cross over itself at point "X". To facilitate tying, the thumb and forefinger of the left hand grasp the line at this point, i.e."X".

Step 2 is simply Step 1 repeated; the thumb and forefinger again assist by holding the two turns at point "X".

In Step 3, a third and final turn (or loop) is formed, the line being returned through the three loops below the standing part. When the end is pulled tight, the loops close on the standing part as in Step 4, and are then pushed down the line to bed against the eye of the hook as in Step 5. The end can then be safely trimmed to within 5 mm of the knot.

If tied as shown, the Centauri Knot will not slip. Tested at 96 per cent of the breaking strength of the line, it is one of the best and easiest knots the author has used. And it is one of the few knots you can easily tie in the dark. Try it.

Line to Line

The Blood Knot (Fig. 7)

The second of the two fundamental knots is the Blood Knot, used for tying or joining two lines together.

Whether the lines are equal or unequal in strength is of little consequence unless, of course, the disparity is exceptional.

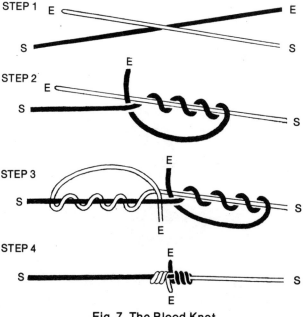

Fig. 7. The Blood Knot

13

The Blood Knot has a knot strength of 77 per cent and, in the author's opinion, is the best and neatest knot for joining nylon lines.

When the ends are trimmed—and this may be done to within 1 mm of the knot—its compactness allows it to pass through rod guides with a minimum of interference. Casts are practically unrestricted as a result, permitting the optimum distance when using a joined line.

Where the diameter of one of the two lines to be joined is much greater than the other, the lesser line should be doubled at the tying end. The angler will rarely encounter this situation, i.e. where the disparity is so great it warrants this procedure. I suppose a parallel would be the tying of a 2-kg line to a 23-kg line. Ask yourself how often you would need to do this.

The Blood Bight Knot (Figs. 8 and 9)

There are many occasions when you will want to fish two or more hooks, e.g. when the whiting are biting, or when you're outside fishing for snapper. Generally speaking, "droppers" are used, i.e. short lengths of line to which the

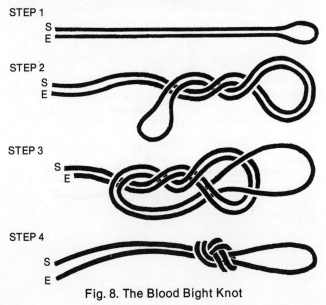

STEP 1

STEP 2

STEP 3

STEP 4

Fig. 8. The Blood Bight Knot

ATTACHING A DROPPER

ATTACHING A SNAPPER LEAD

Fig. 9. The Blood Bight Knot in use

hook is attached, the whole being secured to the main line at varying distances above the sinker.

If you wish, you can attach these droppers to swivels or brass rings spaced above the sinker, by using the Half Blood Knot.

A quicker approach, involving less knots, is to fasten them to loops tied in the main line itself. The Blood Bight Knot is the one you should learn for this, as it has a knot strength of 92 per cent. Fig. 8 illustrates how you can tie this knot. Fig. 9 shows how the loop stands out from the main line. The same knot can be tied at the end of the dropper.

If the loop formed by the Blood Bight Knot is large enough, snapper leads can similarly be quickly attached (see Fig. 9).

Line to Reel

Whilst much care is taken by the average angler when tying nylon to the hook, ring, swivel, etc., many are unsure of the best way to fasten nylon to the spool of a reel. Yet this is an extremely important process, despite the fact that only a

15

handful of fishermen have watched, with growing anxiety, the line disappearing in great handfuls as a big mulloway heads for the far point! Under these conditions the thought may pass through the mind: "Have I tied the end of the line to the spool properly?" If you have, and your luck holds, you may be able to turn that fish at the last moment.

But what about the situation where that $80.00 reel falls from the rod and disappears into the depths? If you grab the line and start pulling, you'll end up with a lot of line in the boat *together with* your reel, *provided the line is tied securely to the spool.* Tie it carelessly and you'll be horrified to see the unattached end of the line come into view.

I have found the following method the most successful, though the Locked Half Blood Knot can also be quite secure.

The knot used to form the loop, is the Blood Bight, which has a knot strength of 92 per cent. This knot is illustrated in Fig. 8.

At first sight, this method may attract criticism; it may be argued that such a tie will slip. Well—provided you have tied it as illustrated, i.e., so that the line is pulling against the loop

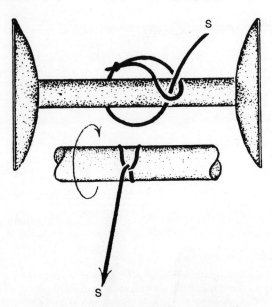

Fig. 10. Tying the line to the reel spool

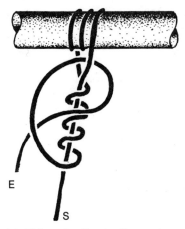

E

S

Fig. 11. Tying the line to the reel spool
using the Locked Half Blood Knot

when the spool (or bail wire) is turned to retrieve line (Fig. 10) *it will not slip*—irrespective of reel type. On the contrary, the stronger the pull, the tighter it will grip the reel spindle or shaft.

Should you prefer the Locked Half Blood Knot, then ensure a non-slip grip by winding the line three times around the spool shaft before tying (Fig. 11).

Float Stop (Fig. 12)

A running float makes for easy casting but, the angler often asks, how to stop it from running right up the line?

Nylon on nylon is the answer, and Fig. 12 illustrates how this is done.

A 15 cm length of monofilament, either of lesser or greater breaking strength than the main line, is tied as shown in Steps 1 and 2.

When pulled tight, the folds grip the main line firmly enough to act as a stop yet not so tightly that the stop cannot be moved, by sliding, along the main line.

When the ends are trimmed to within a millimetre, this stop will pass unimpeded through the rod guides, yet effectively prevent travel of the float beyond it.

It may be necessary to pinch the top eye of the float a little to prevent the knot passing through it.

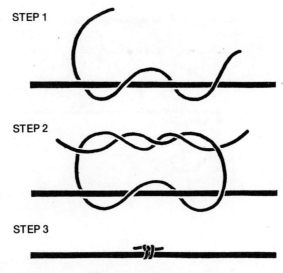

STEP 1

STEP 2

STEP 3

Fig. 12. A stop for floats

Fly-Fishing Knots

About now, the trout enthusiast will be complaining that it appears he is going to be overlooked. To placate him, the following knots are included.

Once again, only the basic knots are sketched, for the author can see no real reason for the inclusion of complicated routines simply for interest purposes. This book is for the practical angler to whom knots are a means to an end.

There are two types of trout angler—the one who spins and the one who fancies fly fishing.

The knots already explained cater for the spinner user, but the fly man has problems which require a daintier approach.

Without becoming involved in a lengthy discourse on fly lines—tapered or level—it will suffice to say that the former, being so expensive and therefore less expendable, must be treated with considerable respect.

The arrangement of a fly line usually comprises backing, tapered line, leader, and fly. The backing can be attached to the reel as illustrated in Fig. 10 or Fig. 11. The attachment of tapered line to backing is quite different.

There are two methods suited to easy tying—(1) the Tucked

Sheet Bend and the Blood Bight and (2) the Tucked Sheet Bend and the Perfection Loop.

For the beginner, method (1) is the simplest, and is commenced by tying the Blood Bight at the free end of the backing. (Fig. 13).

The loop so formed should be of a size commensurate with good judgement but, as a guide, should have a diameter of about 2 cm. The tapered line is then attached using the Tucked Sheet Bend as shown in Fig. 13.

Fig. 13. The Tucked Sheet Bend

Precisely the same processes can be applied when connecting leader and tapered line, except that where the factory produced leaders are used, you will be saved the trouble of tying the Blood Bight.

The Perfection Loop (Fig. 14), though a little more difficult to tie than the Blood Bight, has the advantage of compactness. It has not the knotted strength of the latter, however, having a knot strength of 60 per cent as compared with the Blood Bight's 92 per cent.

Attachment of the fly to the leader must be neatly accomplished, otherwise the dry fly may not sit on the water as naturally as the angler would wish.

A poorly tied knot or a knot of the wrong type could lay the fly on its side or back, thus voiding any semblance to the real insect it was made to imitate.

The inference here is that the type of knot used does not matter greatly when a *wet fly* is fished.

This is fairly true, since a wet fly, mostly imitative of a drowned insect, can be expected to be tossed about and rolled over as it is pushed along by the current..Its "riding" position need not be as immaculately maintained as that of the dry fly.

The Turle Knot (Fig. 15), baby brother of the Two-Circle Turle Knot, is extremely simple to tie, but is one of the weakest and should be avoided wherever possible. The Double Turle Knot shown in Fig. 16 is only slightly stronger and likewise should be avoided. For those who wish to experiment with the Turle Knots, however, take care to leave the running or free end a little longer than most other knots—say, about 5 mm. If this is not done, the thumb knot could work loose.

Many knots have been recommended for this purpose but

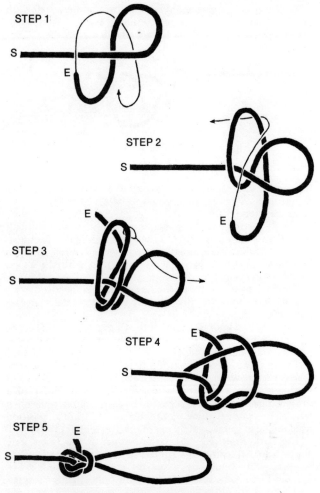

Fig. 14. The Perfection Loop

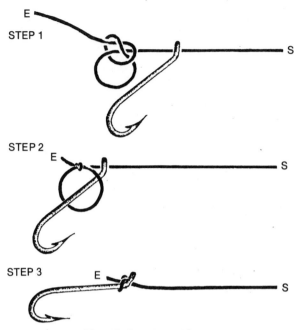

STEP 1

STEP 2

STEP 3

Fig. 15. The Turle Knot

there is only one really effective knot for attaching tippet to fly, whether wet or dry. This is the Locked Half Blood Knot (Fig. 2). It can be used with either the turned up, turned down, or straight eyed hook and, when pulled tight, is neater, stronger, and more efficient than any other. It can also be trimmed closer than most other knots which helps make the fly sit prettier on the water.

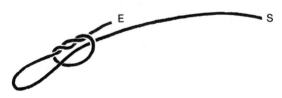

Fig. 16. The Double Turle Knot

The Nail Knot (Fig. 17)

So named because a nail was originally used in forming it, this is an excellent knot for attaching the tapered line to the backing.

Instead of using a nail, however, it is easier to use a piece of plastic tubing about 5 cm long, and the tubing I use is simply a cleaned section cut from a ball-point pen refill. To clean the ink residue from inside the tube, soak a small piece of rag in methylated spirits, attach the rag to a loop in the end of a length of nylon, thread the line through the tube, then pull the rag through as you would when cleaning a rifle barrel.

The knot is then tied as indicated in the illustrations. As Step 1 shows, the tapered line, tube and folded backing line lie parallel to each other. Then (Step 2) the running end of the backing line is wrapped around the tapered line, the tube, and its own standing part, at least six times—preferably eight. Next (Step 3) the running end is passed down through the centre of the tube until it emerges from the opposite end when,

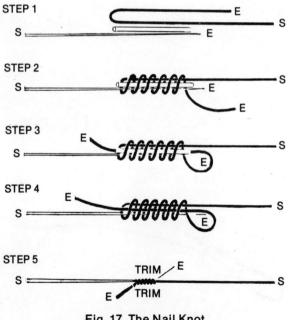

Fig. 17. The Nail Knot

22

by grasping both it AND the tube, it is pulled through the centre of the turns.

The next step is the most difficult, and you can only become efficient at it through experience. Holding the turns between thumb and forefinger of the right hand, discard the plastic tube and slowly, carefully, and firmly, pull on both running end and standing part until the turns tighten on the tapered line.

Trim the tapered line and backing to within 2 mm of the knot and the task is complete. The knot should then be compact and small enough to slip through the snake guides without catching on them.

2 Fishing Rigs

Having mastered the foregoing knots, the reader is invited to put them to the test with the following rigs. These rigs are intended as a guide only; experimenting with your own is most definitely recommended.

BREAM
Beach

NYLON, 5-7 kg   SWIVEL   60 cm

RUNNING
SINKER

HOOK, 1/0-3/0

Rocks

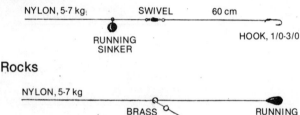

NYLON, 5-7 kg

BRASS
RINGS

RUNNING
SINKER

HOOK, 1/0-3/0

Estuary

NYLON, 2-5 kg

HOOK, 1/0-2/0

WHITING

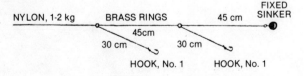

NYLON, 1-2 kg   BRASS RINGS   45 cm   FIXED SINKER

45cm

30 cm   30 cm

HOOK, No. 1   HOOK, No. 1

LEATHERJACKET

Outside

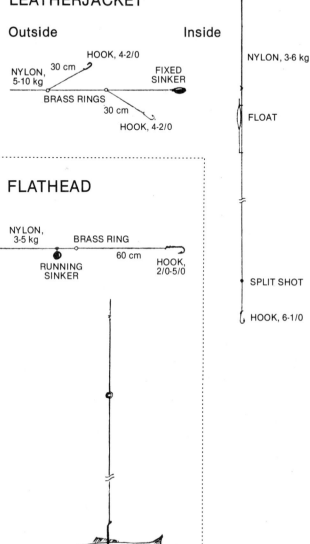

HOOK, 4-2/0

NYLON, 5-10 kg

30 cm

BRASS RINGS

FIXED SINKER

Inside

NYLON, 3-6 kg

FLOAT

30 cm

HOOK, 4-2/0

FLATHEAD

NYLON, 3-5 kg

BRASS RING

60 cm

RUNNING SINKER

HOOK, 2/0-5/0

SPLIT SHOT

HOOK, 6-1/0

LIVE BAIT

LUDERICK

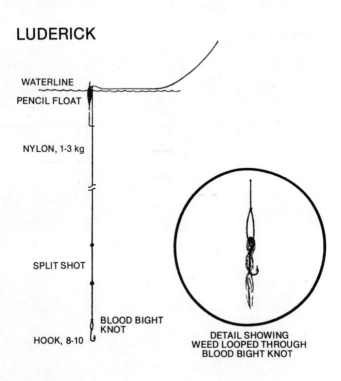

WATERLINE

PENCIL FLOAT

NYLON, 1-3 kg

SPLIT SHOT

BLOOD BIGHT KNOT

HOOK, 8-10

DETAIL SHOWING
WEED LOOPED THROUGH
BLOOD BIGHT KNOT

GARFISH

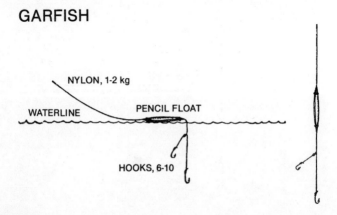

NYLON, 1-2 kg

WATERLINE

PENCIL FLOAT

HOOKS, 6-10

MULLOWAY

NYLON, 5-12 kg   SWIVEL   KEEPER HOOK

RUNNING SINKER   60 cm   HOOK, 2/0-9/0

NYLON, 5-12 kg   SWIVEL   60 cm   HOOKS, 2/0-9/0

RUNNING SINKER   KEEPER HOOK

DRUMMER

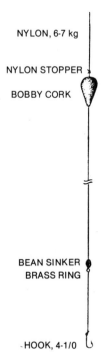

NYLON, 6-7 kg

NYLON STOPPER

BOBBY CORK

BEAN SINKER
BRASS RING

HOOK, 4-1/0

TAILOR

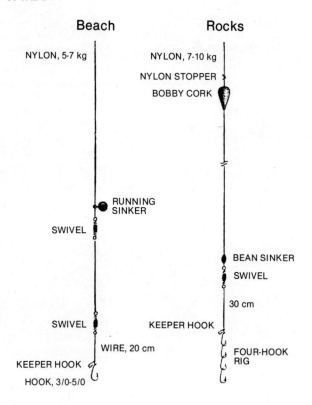

Beach   Rocks

NYLON, 5-7 kg

NYLON, 7-10 kg

NYLON STOPPER

BOBBY CORK

RUNNING SINKER

SWIVEL

BEAN SINKER

SWIVEL

30 cm

SWIVEL

KEEPER HOOK

WIRE, 20 cm

FOUR-HOOK RIG

KEEPER HOOK

HOOK, 3/0-5/0

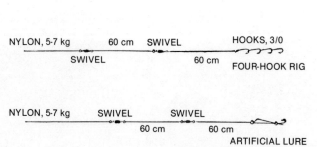

NYLON, 5-7 kg   60 cm   SWIVEL   HOOKS, 3/0

SWIVEL   60 cm   FOUR-HOOK RIG

NYLON, 5-7 kg   SWIVEL   SWIVEL

60 cm   60 cm

ARTIFICIAL LURE

SNAPPER

Rocks

NYLON, 7-10 kg
SWIVEL
BRASS RINGS
60 cm
RUNNING SINKER
45 cm
HOOKS, 3/0-8/0

Outside

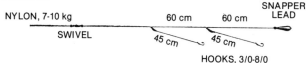

NYLON, 7-10 kg
SWIVEL
60 cm
60 cm
SNAPPER LEAD
45 cm
45 cm
HOOKS, 3/0-8/0

HAIRTAIL

NYLON, 5-7 kg
CURTAIN RING
WIRE, 20 cm
HOOK, 3/0

SALMON

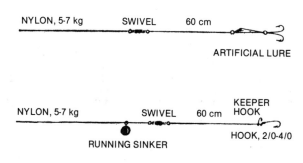

NYLON, 5-7 kg
SWIVEL
60 cm
ARTIFICIAL LURE

NYLON, 5-7 kg
RUNNING SINKER
SWIVEL
60 cm
KEEPER HOOK
HOOK, 2/0-4/0

KINGFISH

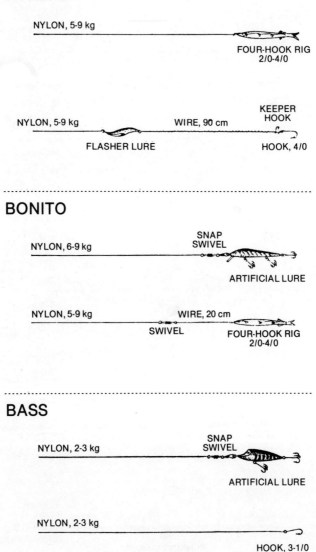

NYLON, 5-9 kg

FOUR-HOOK RIG
2/0-4/0

NYLON, 5-9 kg   WIRE, 90 cm   KEEPER HOOK

FLASHER LURE   HOOK, 4/0

BONITO

NYLON, 6-9 kg   SNAP SWIVEL

ARTIFICIAL LURE

NYLON, 5-9 kg   WIRE, 20 cm

SWIVEL   FOUR-HOOK RIG
2/0-4/0

BASS

NYLON, 2-3 kg   SNAP SWIVEL

ARTIFICIAL LURE

NYLON, 2-3 kg

HOOK, 3-1/0

TROUT

Trolling

NYLON, 2-5 kg SNAP SWIVELS SNAP SWIVEL

KEEL SPINNER

Spinning

NYLON, 1-3 kg SNAP SWIVEL

SPINNER

Using a Fly

TAPERED LINE LEADER

TUCKED SHEET BEND KNOT FLY

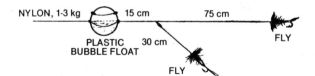

NYLON, 1-3 kg 15 cm 75 cm

PLASTIC BUBBLE FLOAT 30 cm FLY

FLY

REDFIN

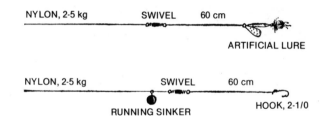

NYLON, 2-5 kg SWIVEL 60 cm

ARTIFICIAL LURE

NYLON, 2-5 kg SWIVEL 60 cm

RUNNING SINKER HOOK, 2-1/0

CALLOP, MURRAY COD

CALLOP—NYLON, 3-5 kg, 1/0-3/0 HOOK

MURRAY COD—NYLON, 7-15 kg, 4/0-8/0 HOOK

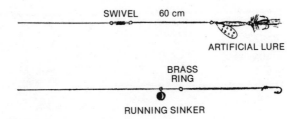

METHODS OF BAITING-UP

Baiting with live prawns.   Baiting with dead prawns.

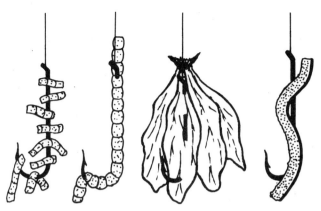

Baiting with worms.

Baiting with sea lettuce.

Baiting with fish flesh.

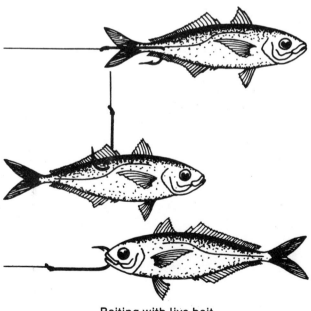

Baiting with live bait.

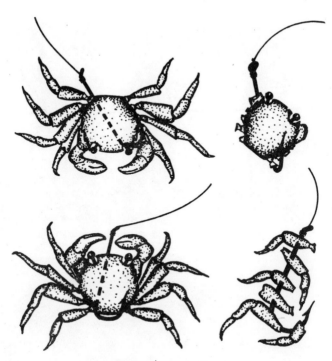

Baiting with crabs.

Baiting, using ganged hooks.

3 · Breaking Strengths

In a series of tests conducted with a nylon monofilament line which, itself, tested at 5.9 kg breaking strength, the following knots reduced the strength of the line to the following percentages of its un-knotted strength.

    (1) Half Blood Knot 96%
    (2) Hangman's Noose 96%
    (3) Blood Bight 92%
    (4) Blood Knot 77%
    (5) Two-Circle Turle Knot 62%

All knots so tested were tied with a dry line.

These percentages should be taken as a guide only. Though each knot was tied and tested several times, the breaking point varied with each tie. The breaking points were averaged, and the percentage then calculated. It is quite possible therefore, for the knot you tie today to be stronger than the same knot tied tomorrow—but only slightly.

Remember, too, that soaking a line for a lengthy period, e.g. an hour or more, can reduce its strength by up to 15 per cent, but usually by about 5 to 10 per cent.

General

The knots described are basically for nylon, easily the most popular line in the world today. Unfortunately, manufacturers have not yet come to an understanding whereby their classifications of line size and breaking strengths are in complete accord—each with the other's. Some breaking strengths quoted are based on their wet strength, i.e. the breaking strength when the line has been soaked in water as when fishing. Others give the dry test strength, whilst still others quote diameter only, although the latter are now rare fortunately.

There are some who will disagree with me on this point (which is healthy, I suppose!) but, no matter what they say or how they argue, discussions with, and letters from, hundreds of practical and not-so-practical anglers overwhelmingly suggest, to me, a bias in favour of the breaking strength being quoted. Line diameter means little to most anglers, though it is a guide, and can help, to estimate how much line a reel of a certain size, can hold.

Nylon lines are sometimes referred to as being "soft". This is a bad word, for nylon lines are invariably hard. What is meant or implied is that the line is limp, or has a certain limpness about it, and these are better ways of describing the pliancy or flexibility of the line. The antonym, I suppose, would be "stiff" or "stiffness".

A stiff nylon line is not a good one—and many cheap lines are stiff. When wound on to a spool they tend to spring from it—whether it be a sidecast, fixed, or overhead type reel. This leads to tangles and backlash and vituperation! It too, has no "give" in it, a very necessary requirement as I will explain shortly.

A limp line, on the other hand, provided it is not so limp it stretches like rubber, is the ideal. It lies well on the spool and will not spring from it when not under tension. It can be stretched as a good line should, but it must not stretch to a point where a strike by an angler merely lengthens the line without setting the hook. Stretch acts as a shock absorber, thus minimising line breakage resulting from the hit or fight of a fast moving powerful fish, but it must be within certain limits.

Too much stretch can ruin a spool as effectively as belting it with a hammer. A line with a lot of stretch, when wound on wet under pressure, can contract as it dries and twist the spool out of shape or force the end plates clear off the shaft. It has happened to me and I know of many anglers who have undergone the same experience.

And so you ask, "How can I tell, when I buy a line, whether it has too much, not enough, or just enough, stretch?"

There is no formula and I must confess it is a most difficult thing to determine. As a guide however I would suggest you take a 60 cm length of say 7 kg breaking strength line, fasten each end to a swivel, and then endeavour to stretch it as far as you can. Eight centimetres of stretch before the line becomes difficult to stretch any further, can be considered reasonable. The line should then return to its original length—give or take a millimetre or two. You will find that most good quality lines give this result.

Nylon lines often break (not at the knot) for no apparent reason—invariably when you have that biggest of big ones on the other end! There are two main reasons for line breakage—other than weakening by knots — and they are abrasion, or weakening by the heat of friction.

Abrasion, is self-explanatory. Rubbing against rocks, being pulled across a sandy bottom, movement through worn and grooved rod guides, etc., can all cause this. Weakening by friction is not so apparent. Try this experiment.

Take a 90 cm length of nylon and fasten one end of it to a nail in the fence. Holding it tight at the other end, rub the line briskly with your handkerchief. In a matter of seconds the line will break like cotton, the heat from the rubbing having disturbed the molecular structure of the nylon to the point where it no longer holds the material together.

How can this ruin your line when fishing?

That's easy!

The angler who uses an overhead reel must always be on guard against backlash, that cursed tangle of the line within the confines of the reel cage. Those who overcome this by thumbing the line on the spool will recall those occasions when they suffered a nasty thumb burn as they pressed their thumb against the line on the rapidly revolving spool. I wonder how many were aware that their line also suffered— from the heat generated, which weakened and frayed the line as it did when you tried the handkerchief test.

Breaking Strengths and Line Diameters

BREAKING STRENGTH (kg)	DIAMETER mm	BREAKING STRENGTH (kg)	DIAMETER mm
.5	.10	20.4	.70
.7	.12	22.7	.75
1.1	.15	27.2	.80
1.6	.17	31.7	.90
2.0	.20	36.3	1.00
2.3	.22	41.7	1.10
2.7	.25	49.9	1.20
3.4	.27	56.7	1.30
4.1	.30	59.0	1.35
5.4	.35	65.8	1.40
6.8	.40	72.6	1.45
8.6	.45	90.7	1.50
10.4	.50	99.8	1.60
12.7	.55	113.4	1.70
14.5	.60	120.2	1.80
16.3	.65	133.8	1.90

The line, pressing against the rod tip guide as it is taken out by a powerful fish, can similarly be weakened. Roller tips reduce this to the point where it is no longer a major worry, but the beach angler doesn't use roller tips as a general rule.

There are few other reasons for line failure. Long exposure to sunlight will have a deteriorating effect and should be avoided, whilst some of the more commonly encountered chemicals will affect nylon at normal temperatures—10-32 degrees Celsius. Dimethylphthalate, the very effective mosquito lotion, will attack it, as will glacial acetic acid, formic acid, hydrogen peroxide, and sulphuric acid.

Despite its high resistance to chemicals, I still prefer to give the line a rinse in fresh water after each outing. This washes away the salt clinging to the line, so preventing it from attacking the metal spool.

If you are in doubt as to the correct breaking strength of a particular line, carry out the following simple test. All you require is a set of pocket scales—the sort with a hook at one end and a ring at the other—and a cup hook. Screw the cup hook into some strong support (a fence post is ideal) and hang the scales on the hook. Select a length of the line to be tested—about 60 cm will be ample—and fasten one end to the hook of the scales with a Half Blood Knot. Then wind seven or eight turns of the line around the same hook so that no turn overlaps. Wind the free end around a pencil and hold tightly so the line will not slip.

Pull the line gradually and watch the dial of the pocket scales, noting the weight registered when the line breaks. The result is the appropriate breaking strength of your line.

The reason for winding the line around the pencil and hook is to avoid any direct pull on a knot which, obviously, is the line's weakest point. If the tension is applied directly to the knot, you will get the actual knot strength of the line.

You can also quickly arrive at a reasonable estimate of a line's breaking strength if you use a micrometer to measure the line diameter. Compare the reading with the diameters shown on the chart and read off the breaking strength.

For example, a line with a diameter of .40 of a millimetre has an approximate breaking strength of 7 kg. Since diameters of lines can vary from manufacturer to manufacturer (for the same breaking strength), the information shown in the chart is not accurate for all lines. However, the diameters shown apply to a well-respected brand, and may be accepted as a basis on which to adjudge most lines.

4 Swivels

In the chapter, "Fishing Rigs", the swivel is shown as common connector between line and leader. This very simple item is so frequently mis-used that the following tips were deemed appropriate for this booklet.

First, it is an established fact that there has not been a swivel made that is 100 per cent effective. Secondly, of all the swivels made, the ball-bearing type is the closest to perfection. It is also the most costly and, for this reason, not as popular as the common box, or barrel, types which, under pressure, are barely 50 per cent effective. A fourth type, the torpedo swivel, is not normally used by the average fisherman, but is popular with the big-game fisherman.

When buying swivels your first rule should be: "The lighter the line, the smaller the swivel".

Too many fishermen work on the assumption that a larger swivel will turn better than a small one. And they sometimes refuse to be convinced otherwise. The shop assistant then withholds further counsel and applies the rule that the customer knows best!

Breaking Strengths and Swivel Sizes

BREAKING STRENGTH	SWIVEL
Up to 3.2 kg	No. 14
3.6-5.4 kg	12 or 11
5.9-7.7 kg	10 or 9
8.2-10 kg	8 or 7
10.4-12.2 kg	6 or 5
12.7-14.5 kg	4 or 3
15-16.8 kg	2 or 1
17.2-20.4 kg	1/0 or 2/0
22.7-31.7 kg	3/0 or 4/0
34-54.4 kg	5/0

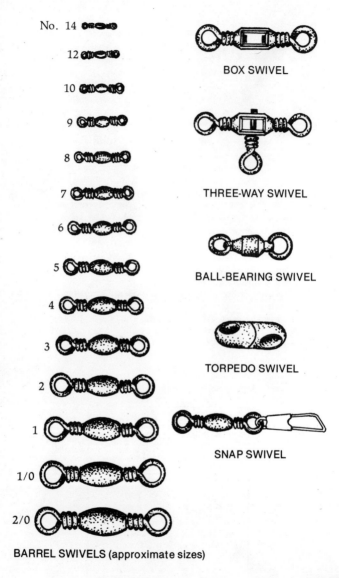

No. 14

12

10

9

8

7

6

5

4

3

2

1

1/0

2/0

BARREL SWIVELS (approximate sizes)

BOX SWIVEL

THREE-WAY SWIVEL

BALL-BEARING SWIVEL

TORPEDO SWIVEL

SNAP SWIVEL

Fig. 18. Swivels for fishing

Try the following experiment. Select two box, or barrel, swivels—a No. 14 and a No. 5. To one end of a metre length of nylon (any breaking strength) tie a 84 g sinker and, to the other end, tie the larger (No. 5) swivel. Let the sinker hang down then spin it between the fingers and watch how effectively it causes the swivel to rotate. Then remove the large swivel, replace it with the smaller (No. 14) and repeat the process. You'll notice how much more effectively the smaller swivel spins. Then tie line and sinker to a ball-bearing swivel and note the big improvement over the other type.

The chart on page 39 will assist you in your choice of swivels.

5   Balanced Tackle

More and more in these enlightened days (fishing days, that is!) we are turning to light tackle so as to increase our fishing fun. And the lighter we go, the greater is the skill required on our part, and the more stress placed on our equipment. The term "balanced tackle" is a much abused one. It does *not* mean that rod and reel swing like a see-saw when laid on your index finger at a certain point along the rod. You could manage that with an expensive game rod and a chain store centre-pin reel—and what a combination that would be!

"Balanced tackle" means that rod, reel, line, lure (or sinker) and rig, are so assembled that they are perfectly matched for the job required of them.

A reel can be balanced with a certain rod; a rod can be balanced with a certain line; and a line can be balanced with a certain wire (or sinker); and they can all be balanced as a whole. But, whereas you can use almost any rod or reel for catching fish, the one thing that remains relatively constant is the line. No matter what the rod or reel, each is useless unless it is married to a line. And, whilst it is important that the line balance fairly well with the rod and suit the reel, it is even more important that the lure to be cast balances with the line. You can experience much difficulty if you are careless in this respect.

Let's assume we're dealing with sinkers, and that you've just taken up beach fishing. You've a well-balanced outfit, consisting of a hollow-glass 4-metre surf rod, an overhead reel correctly spooled with 7 kg breaking strength nylon monofilament and located about 70 cm from the butt, and you're bait-fishing for bream. You're using a 2-kg leader because you're a light-tackle enthusiast. What would be the best weight to tie to your line to allow you to cast out to where the bream are feeding?

Either a 70 or 84 g sinker, attached to the main line above the leader, would permit optimum casting.

If you only had a 14 g sinker in your tackle box, you'd be in bother for you'd find it almost impossible to cast any significant distance. The light weight would be insufficient to pull that 7 kg line from the spool and through the runners, regardless of how much muscle you put into the cast. If, on the other hand, you'd spooled that reel with 2 kg line, then neither the 14 g nor the 84 g sinker would be satisfactory. You would get very little distance with the former, whilst the weight of the latter, due to the force applied by the caster, necessary to start the spool rolling, would surely snap the light line.

The solution here is to attach a 7 kg leader—say 5 m in length—to the light line (with the Blood Knot, Fig. 7) and use the heavier sinker. The strain will be taken by the heavier line and the lighter line will follow.

If you're competition fishing, make sure the length of that leader conforms with the rules. A leader of reasonable length should not exceed, in length, one and a half times the length of the rod.

Line and lure matching becomes even more critical when ultra-light weights are used. The trout fisherman, with his 2 g and 3 g spinners, well knows the impracticability of using 7 kg breaking strength lines with such light lures.

Even with a thread-line reel, where there is no spool to start turning—where the line simply peels over the lip of the spool—distance can drop astonishingly when there's a significant increase in line breaking strength over lure weight. Those light lures have not the weight to pull the heavy line for any distance—no matter what rod is used or how well it is made or who is using it. For such light lures, lines of 1 to 2 kg breaking strength are good, whilst a 1 kg breaking strength line will be better and really test your fishing skill.

Of course, once you get down as light as this you'll find your choice of reel is restricted to the thread-line type. Bait-casters are "out", for the featherlights lack the weight to turn the spool and keep pulling line from it. The average single-handed bait-caster works best with lines of 2 to 3 kg and lures from 7 to 28 g.

Even the thread-line reel will work poorly if underfilled or overfilled with line. It is often claimed that backlash is impossible with a thread-line reel—and this is quite correct, too. But substitute the word "bird's nest" for "backlash" (they're frequently used synonymously) and the claim is completely invalid, for you can get an even worse "bird's nest" with a thread-line than you can with a bait-caster or overhead reel simply by winding too much line on the spool.

The thread-line spool should be filled within 2 mm of the lip.

If you fill it flush with the lip, your first cast will invite that cursed bird's nest. Instead of the one loop being followed successively by a series of loops that flow smoothly through the runners, a dozen or more will be encouraged to do so at the one time. As they all try to squeeze through that bottom runner together, chaos will ensue with the obvious result.

Underfill the spool, e.g., half fill it, and the drag of the line over the lip will reduce your distance. That 2 mm has been found the ideal, so stay with it.

The following chart shows recommended lure-sinker weights for use with lines of various breaking strengths:

Breaking Strengths and Lure-Sinker Weights

BREAKING STRENGTH	LURE-SINKER WEIGHT
.45 kg	to 7 g
.9 kg	7 g
1.4 kg	14 g
2.3 kg	17 g
3.2 kg	21 g
4.1 kg	28 g
5.4 kg	56 g
6.8 kg	84 g
8.2 kg	112 g
9.5 kg	112 g
11.3 kg	168 g

6 Fly Lines

Earlier, we discussed the need for balancing line breaking strength with lure weight, and came to the rather obvious conclusion that, to cast any distance, the spin-fisherman needed a lure, or sinker, heavy enough to pull the line behind it. How then is it possible to cast a lure any distance when it is practically weightless?

The fly fisherman is faced with this problem every day of his fishing life. He solves it, most satisfactorily, by using a line that has sufficient weight to pull itself, with assistance from rod and user, through the air and, in so doing, tow that almost weightless lure, a fly, behind.

Very generally speaking, weight is imparted to the fly line either by coating a level braided core (which, in itself, can vary in size and weight) with PVC plastic or, in the case of a braided line, by varying the number and thickness of the strands of yarn used to make it.

To suit various conditions, e.g., windy, lake, or stream, which govern distance and water fished, fly lines are given shape as well as length and these shapes are given names by which the line is known. There are four basic shapes: the level, double taper, forward taper, and shooting taper, and each can be made to float or sink. A profile of each can be seen in Fig. 19.

To make it easy for the fly fisherman to choose an appropriate line, manufacturers have universally agreed to a code that is usually printed on the box in which the line is packed. A double taper line that floats might, for instance, be coded as a "DT 6 F" line. The "DT" stands for "double taper"; the digit 6 for the weight of the line (see below); and the "F" signifies that the line floats. A sinking, weight-forward line of the same weight as the DT 6 F would carry the code "WF 6 S".

The digit, in both instances, is a code in itself, for it indicates the weight in grains of the first 9.1 m of the line from the beginning of the taper. In other words, the first 9.1 m of taper of the DT 6 F line would weigh 160 grains. The following codes are standard throughout the world:

Fly Line Coding

LINE (No.)	WEIGHT (GRAINS)
1	60
2	80
3	100
4	120
5	140
6	160
7	185
8	210
9	240
10	280
11	330
12	380

For most Australian streams, lines of 140, 160, and 185 grains—or codes 5, 6 and 7 respectively—are the ideal.

Fly lines, used in salt-water fly fishing, are usually heavier and vary from 210 grains up to 380 grains.

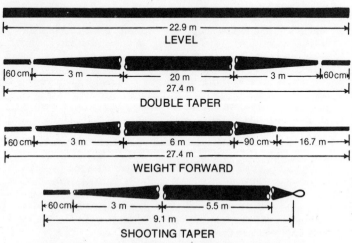

Fig. 19. The basic shapes of fly lines

The Fly Line Leader

Since the bulk of a fly line can frighten a fish as it hits the water, and since this bulk makes it practically impossible to pass the end through the eye of a fly hook, a nylon leader is used. It provides an almost invisible link between the fly and the fly line.

Fly line leaders are normally tapered—the thick end (or "butt") being attached to the fly line, and the thin end (or "tippet") to the fly. They are made in various lengths, the two most popular being 2.3 m and 2.7 m.

As with ordinary nylon monofilament, leaders can be bought in various breaking strengths, the thin end or tippet being the section to which the quoted breaking strength applies. Once again a code is used:

Fly Line Leader Coding

CODE	BREAKING STRENGTH	HOOK SIZE
7X	453 g	18 through to 28
6X	860 g	14, 16, 18, or 20
5X	1.3 kg	12, 14, 16, or 18
4X	1.7 kg	12, 14, or 16
3X	2.2 kg	8, 10, 12, or 14
2X	2.6 kg	6, 8, or 10
1X	3.2 kg	4, 6, or 8
0X	3.9 kg	1, 2, 4, or 6
8/5	5.0 kg	1/0 upwards
6/5	6.4 kg	1/0 upwards

The light-tackle exponent can still ease his conscience by using a 7X leader, whereas the gourmet might choose a 1X! Since the fly fisherman makes use of hooks that vary from the smallest in the world, up to and beyond the common No. 1 and 1/0, his choice of fly governs his choice of leader, for the eyes of the smaller hooks are too small to accept lines of large diameter. The above chart also serves as a guide to the correct hook size.

7 Game-Fishing Knots and Wire Rigs

This book would be incomplete if we ignored the use of wire in fishing, for, just as there are special knots for nylon, so it is important that a wire trace be correctly secured to the hook, swivel, or ring.

Whilst beyond the intended scope of this book, some knots used in game fishing will be of interest to many anglers, also.

The following knots are used with braided Dacron and are used (1) to form the large loop which is known as the "double" and (2) to attach the double to the swivel.

The length of the double is 9.14 m for lines up to and including 60 kg breaking strength.

It is, in effect, a trace, but should not be confused with the wire trace between hook and swivel.

The ties are accomplished as follows:

The Double Tie (Fig. 20)

Having determined the length of the "double", or "loop", throw a hitch around the standing part as shown in Step 1.

Then, holding the loop and running end between thumb and forefinger of one hand, twist the double twice as shown in Step 2.

Next (Step 3), pass the running end down between the double strands and commence to plait, tightly, the three lengths of line thus formed.

Continue to plait for approximately 5 cm and finish by looping the running end around one side of the double as shown in Step 5, and pulling tight.

The running end should then be threaded back through the woven strands for about 2 cm as in Steps 5 and 6.

Double to Swivel (Fig. 21)

The running end of the double, having been passed through the swivel ring, is bent back along itself and looped as in Step 1 (Fig. 21).

The running end is then wound four times around the four strands (now the standing part) thus formed, care being taken to keep the windings within the loop formed (Step 2).

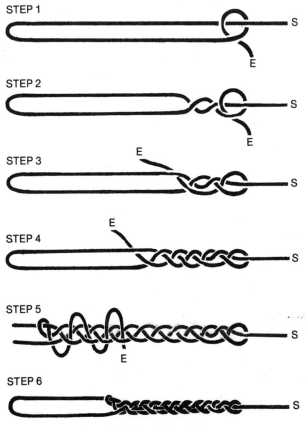

STEP 1

STEP 2

STEP 3

STEP 4

STEP 5

STEP 6

Fig. 20. Double steps

By holding the swivel and strands in the left hand and pulling carefully on the running end, the knot is drawn tight. You can then slide it down on to the swivel as in Step 3.

This knot is similar to the Hangman's Noose.

Wire Rigs

Despite the availability of crimping tools and sleeves, there are still many anglers who find the expense of these unwarranted.

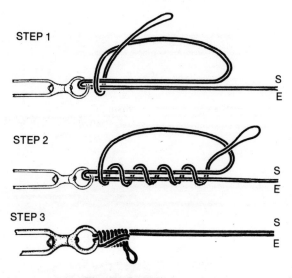

STEP 1

STEP 2

STEP 3

Fig. 21. Double to swivel

True, one can, for a very small sum, purchase nylon covered traces ready rigged with swivels and snap catch which, for certain purposes, are excellent. There will, however, always be anglers who will need to "tie their own" (the author is one of these) and for them the following tie is recommended.

The Lewers Wire Tie (Figs. 22 and 23)

Specially designed for nylon covered wire which is harder to tie than plain wire, the Lewers Wire Tie can be used, with equal facility, for the latter.

At first sight, the tying may seem complicated, but don't let that deter you. You need only tie it once to master it; thereafter, I am sure it will serve you well, for I have never had it fail me.

Steps 1 and 2 (Fig. 23) are self-explanatory. It is important, however, that upon the completion of Step 2, the knot so formed be drawn as tight as possible, as in Step 3.

You will then find it a simple matter to slide the knot along the standing part until it beds against the brass ring, or swivel, etc.

You conclude the tie by winding the running end around the standing part, four times, tucking it under on the final turn as shown in Step 5. The excess can then be snipped off to within 2 mm.

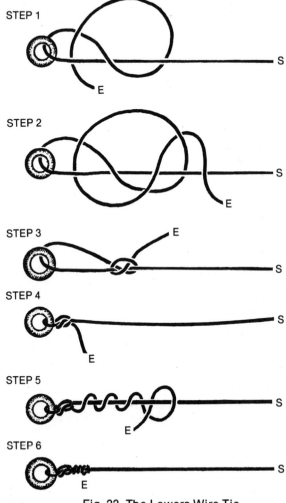

STEP 1

STEP 2

STEP 3

STEP 4

STEP 5

STEP 6

Fig. 22. The Lewers Wire Tie

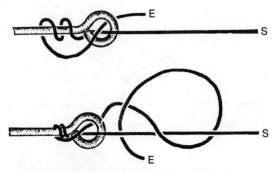

(CONTINUE AS WITH STEPS 1 TO 6 OF FIG. 22)

Fig. 23. The Lewers Wire Tie for hooks

Note that the turns are made around the standing part which should remain straight throughout. If the turns are wound tightly, the finished tie will be neat and tidy as in Step 6.

Fig. 23 illustrates how this tie can be used when attaching a hook to wire. Having gone as far as Step 2 (Fig. 23) continue as with Steps 1 to 6 (Fig. 22).

The complete tie is as shown in Fig. 23.

Wire to Lure

When attaching a lure to a wire trace, care must be taken to ensure that action of the lure is not impeded by the stiffness and tightness of the wire tie.

Where a lure is attached to a snap swivel, the Lewers Wire Tie to the swivel will be found the most efficient but, where the wire is tied directly to the lure, another method must be used.

If the wire is looped as shown in Fig. 24 (Steps 1 and 2), this free movement will be facilitated.

In the illustration, the running end is shown bound to the standing part with thin copper wire, the bound section being soldered for complete security. Of course, those who own a crimping tool will not have to resort to this.

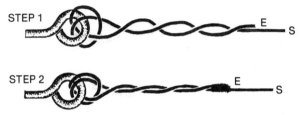

STEP 1

STEP 2

Fig. 24. Wire to lure

For clarity, a hook eye is shown in the illustration. This could, however, be the leading ring of a jig or spinner.

The length of wire to use with lures and hooks is a controversial subject. Experience has shown me that rarely indeed is a lure swallowed whole, thus bringing the line into contact with the fish's mouth. I seldom, as a result, use wire when trolling or spinning, and only occasionally it is necessary when bait fishing. Two fish really worthy of wire are the tailor and the hairtail, and for these the minimum length should, for real safety, be 20 cm between hook eye and swivel.

Light game fishermen who tangle with tuna and large kingfish, etc., sometimes use wire leaders of 1, 2, or more metres in length. This obviates line damage through contact with the fish's body, though often, a heavier leader than the main line will suffice.

8 Nautical Knots

Boating and fishing go hand in hand. So why not, in a book on angling knots, illustrate knots that will be of use to the boating angler?

Here is the first—an appropriate knot in the circumstances.

The Fisherman's Bend (Fig. 25)

When fastening (or "bending", if you're nautically bent!) a rope to the ring of an anchor, the Fisherman's Bend is as good as any knot for the purpose.

Fig. 25 illustrates this clearly. When drawn tight, the running end should then be seized to the standing part for greater security.

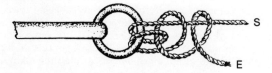

Fig. 25. The Fisherman's Bend

"Seizing" is the process of binding together with strong thread or light rope, two ropes or two parts of the same rope. It may also be known as "stopping back". The procedure is uncomplicated as can be seen from Fig. 26.

Fig. 26. Seizing

Making fast to an object with a rope is dependent upon the circumstances. If it is to a ring, either at the bow or stern of the boat, then the aforementioned Fisherman's Bend is appropriate.

If you wish to make fast to a post or bollard, then you have three more choices—the Round Turn and Two Half Hitches, the Bowline, and the Clove Hitch.

There are others of course, but the above three are sufficient for the fussiest angler. Here they are:

Round Turn and Two Half Hitches (Fig. 27)

Its formation is easy to follow from the illustration (Fig. 27). The turn around the post takes most of the strain. As a

Fig. 27. A Round Turn and two Half Hitches

result, the two half hitches do not harden as much as they might, which facilitates release when time to cast off.

The Bowline (Fig. 28)

This is the most useful way to tie a fixed loop in the end of the rope. It will not slip, and the loop can simply be dropped over the post or bollard. It can be tied beforehand too, which can make for safer and quicker tying up.

Commence the tie by forming a half hitch at the required distance from the end of the rope, pass the end through the loop formed, then take it behind and around the standing part bringing it back down through the loop again.

Tighten by pulling the standing part with the left hand and the loop and running end with the right hand.

Fig. 28. The Bowline

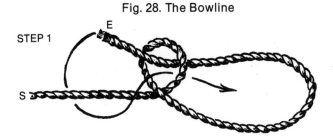

STEP 1

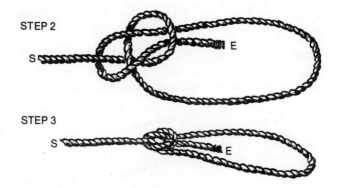

STEP 2

S

E

STEP 3

S

E

The Clove Hitch (Fig. 29)

This knot is often used by anglers to make fast to a post or bollard. For this purpose, it is not as satisfactory as the Bowline or the Round Turn and two Half Hitches—the motion of the boat in rough water can gradually work it slack.

S

E

Fig. 29. The Clove Hitch

If you wish to use it, however, give yourself permanent security by hitching the running end to the standing part with two Half Hitches pulled tight. Then it is as good as any knot, and very secure.

Splicing

The Eye Splice (Fig. 30)

Unlay (unravel) for a short distance the three strands that form the rope and, after forming the loop to the required size, tuck the middle or No. 2 strand under one of the strands of the

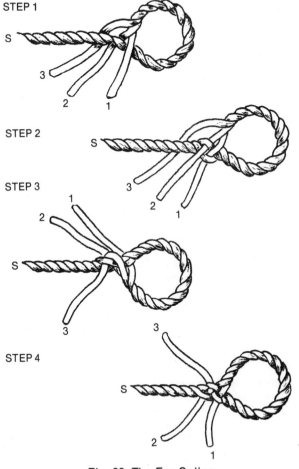

Fig. 30. The Eye Splice

standing part as shown in Step 1. At this point, Strand 3 should be under the rope, with Strand 1 on top.

With the aid of a spike, lift the next adjacent strand of the standing part and tuck Strand No. 1 under it as shown in Step 2.

Now turn the loop over so that Strand 3 lies atop it, and tuck this under the only other strand that has nothing under it.

Note that the direction appears to have been reversed and that all strands have been tucked at the same point on the rope.

Taking each of Strands 1, 2 and 3, in turn, continue to tuck them under succeeding strands (Step 4) until they are used up.

A tapered appearance can be given the splice by halving the strands before the last couple of tucks, the unwanted strands being cut off and the remainder carried on to the finish.

It is always a good idea to whip the ends of the strands before starting the splice, and just after halving near the finish but before severing the unwanted halves.

This makes the strands easier to handle and helps prevent them working out of the finished job.

The Short Splice (Fig. 31)

As with the Eye Splice, each rope should be unravelled for the required length and then crotched so that the strands of one rope go alternately between those of the other as in Step 1. In actual practice they should be hard up against one another; they are shown apart for the sake of clarity.

Each unravelled strand should be tucked over one strand of the standing part and under the next, the process being repeated for each, and until all are used up.

When finished, the splice can be rolled between the palms of the hand or under foot to even up the strands and round the whole neatly.

Common Whipping (Fig. 32)

Anyone who has made a rod or bound a runner to a rod will be familiar with whipping. Whipping the end of a rope can be an exactly similar process, or it can vary according to the whim of the person concerned. Its purpose is to prevent the end of the rope fraying or unravelling.

The number of turns comprising the whipping should be at least equal to, or greater than, the diameter of the rope.

The process is extremely simple. Lay one end of the whip-

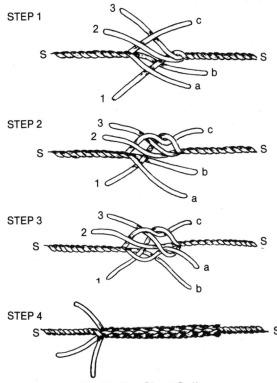

STEP 1

STEP 2

STEP 3

STEP 4

Fig. 31. The Short Splice

ping twine along the rope and wind a number of turns around it as shown in Step 1. Draw these as tight as possible, then lay the other end of the twine along the rope in the opposite direction and wind more tight turns over it as in Step 2. Finally, pull end "A" (Step 3) tight against the last turn formed, and cut off close. The finished whipping should appear as in Step 4.

It is always a good idea to wax the whipping twine and this can be done by drawing it through a knob of beeswax.

Sailmaker's Whipping (Fig. 33)

This is perhaps the most secure whipping. After waxing the whipping twine, unlay the end strands of the rope for about

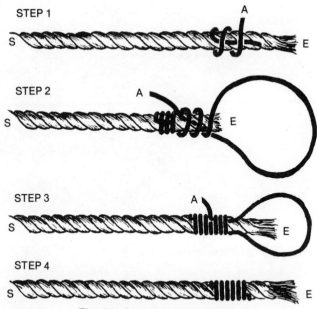

Fig. 32. Common Whipping

4 cm, and loop the twine over strand "X" as shown in Step 1.

Grasp the loop and short end "N" and, holding them against the rope, wind on the required number of turns with the long end "L". Then lift the loop over the strand "X" (Step 2) and pull the short ends "N" until the loop beds tightly over the turns.

Taking the ends "L" and "N", tie them tightly together, with a reef knot, in the centre of the unravelled ends.

Trim the ends to complete the whipping.

Making Fast (Fig. 34)

I wonder how many boat fishermen know the correct way of tying their painter to a cleat. Do you, for example, toss on half a dozen half hitches and leave it at that? Or a series of figure-eights?

The steps shown in Fig. 34 depict the correct way to cleat or make fast. The main object is to ensure that the rope will not jam should it be necessary to cast off in a hurry.

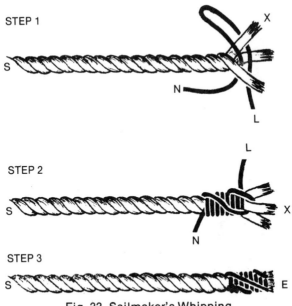

Fig. 33. Sailmaker's Whipping

In Step 1, the running end is taken around the cleat on the side opposite the strain. This is important. It is then continued on around the stem of the cleat, under the horn to the other side, and brought back over the centre, as in Step 2.

A loop is then formed in the running end (Step 3) and slipped over the other horn. Repeat the process over and under each horn several times (Fig. 4) when it will hold securely until ready to cast off.

As your life could depend on the condition of your anchor rope, care should be taken to protect it from damage or deterioration.

Whilst synthetic fibres are becoming increasingly popular, the old standby, Manila rope, continues to be favoured by thousands of boat owners. The fibres from which this rope is made come from a plant called "abaca", and in their raw state contain a natural oil which helps to protect them from the elements. During manufacture, more oils are added but, through repeated exposure to weather and immersion in water, these oils leach away and the rope becomes more susceptible to rot.

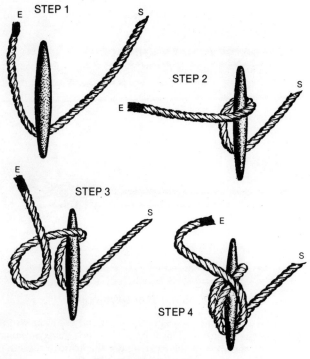

Fig. 34. Making fast

Rot is caused by a fungus which flourishes where there is moisture. Never, therefore, stow your Manila rope away wet. Thorough drying in the sun after each outing will prolong its life considerably but, if you really care, wash it in fresh water to remove any salt and then dry.

Kinks and twists and tangles can damage the fibres particularly if strain is put on a rope with these present. Always coil the rope neatly so it will run free when needed.

Synthetic fibres such as polypropylene and polyethylene make excellent ropes. For all practical purposes they are unaffected by prolonged immersion in water whether salt or fresh. They are lighter than sea water and, if lost overboard, will float until retrieved. They hold less water which means a drier boat when the anchor is hauled aboard, and they offer good resistance to sunlight.

Generally speaking, the author prefers them to the heavier Manila rope for reasons of lightness, strength, and resistance to deterioration.

Polyethylene Rope Tying

Since modern materials have given us braided polyethylene ropes for use as anchor ropes, it is useful to know the different, more simple, method of splicing them. The procedure for forming a loop in the end of such a rope is as follows:

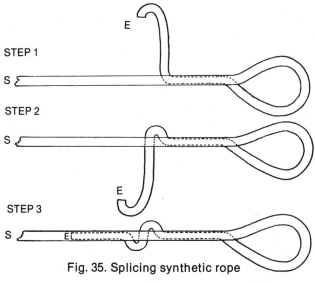

Fig. 35. Splicing synthetic rope

Firstly, prevent the loose ends of the rope from unravelling by melting them with a match or wrapping with adhesive tape. The former is best since all the ends will be fused together. Determine the size of the loop required, and prize apart the strands of the rope at the point along its length where the loop is to commence. At this point insert the running end into the hollow centre or core of the rope and, with the fingers, work it along within the core for a good 15 cm. Then prize the strands apart as before and pull the running end through (Step 1).

One or two strands away from this point of exit, pass the running end clear through the rope and pull it tight (Step 2). Once again, one or two strands away from this latter point of exit, re-insert the running end in the core and work it along to its limit (Step 3). Roll the splice between the palms of your hands to smooth it out, and the task is complete.

Joining Synthetic Ropes (Fig. 36)

The joining of two ropes is accomplished in a similar fashion.

Commence by laying the running ends of each rope side by side so that each overlaps the other by about 60 cm.

At point "W" on Rope B (Fig. 36) prize the strands apart and insert, as far as point "X", end "Z" of Rope A. Work end "Z" along for approximately 15 cm, then prize the strands apart as before and pull end "Z" through.

Re-insert end "Z" one or two strands away from its point of exit, passing it clear through the rope. One or two strands further along Rope B, insert end "Z" into the core again and work it along to its limit. Repeating the process for end "Y" and Rope A (Steps 3, 4) and rolling between the hands as before completes the splice.

The above procedure can be followed when joining or forming into a loop, braided Dacron or braided nylon lines. Because of their fine diameter however, a needle or very fine wire must be used to pull the ends through the hollow centre.

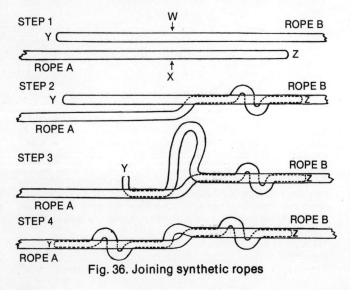

Fig. 36. Joining synthetic ropes